OWNER AND VEHICLE INFORMATION

Name: ______________________

Address: ______________________

Business Address: ______________________

Model: ______________________ Make: ______________________

Vin: ______________________

Purchase Date: ______________________ From: ______________________

Dealer Info: ______________________

Insurance Company: ______________________

Agent: ______________________

Phone: ______________________

Notes: ______________________

Year:________________ Make:________________ Model:________________

Date/Time	Odometer		Total Mileage	Destination	Notes
	Start	End			

Year:________________ Make:________________ Model:________________

Date/Time	Odometer		Total Mileage	Destination	Notes
	Start	End			

Year:________________ Make:________________ Model:________________

Date/Time	Odometer		Total Mileage	Destination	Notes
	Start	End			

Year:______________ Make:______________ Model:______________

Date/Time	Odometer		Total Mileage	Destination	Notes
	Start	End			

Year:________________ Make:________________ Model:________________

Date/Time	Odometer		Total Mileage	Destination	Notes
	Start	End			

Year:________________ Make:________________ Model:________________

Date/Time	Odometer		Total Mileage	Destination	Notes
	Start	End			

Year:________________ Make:________________ Model:________________

Date/Time	Odometer		Total Mileage	Destination	Notes
	Start	End			

Year:________________ Make:________________ Model:________________

Date/Time	Odometer		Total Mileage	Destination	Notes
	Start	End			

Year:________________ Make:________________ Model:________________

Date/Time	Odometer		Total Mileage	Destination	Notes
	Start	End			

Year:____________ Make:____________ Model:____________

Date/Time	Odometer		Total Mileage	Destination	Notes
	Start	End			

Year:________________ Make:________________ Model:________________

Date/Time	Odometer		Total Mileage	Destination	Notes
	Start	End			

Year:________________ Make:________________ Model:________________

Date/Time	Odometer		Total Mileage	Destination	Notes
	Start	End			

Year:________________ Make:________________ Model:________________

Date/Time	Odometer		Total Mileage	Destination	Notes
	Start	End			

Year:________________ Make:________________ Model:________________

Date/Time	Odometer		Total Mileage	Destination	Notes
	Start	End			

Year:_______________ Make:_______________ Model:_______________

Date/Time	Odometer		Total Mileage	Destination	Notes
	Start	End			

Year:________________ Make:________________ Model:________________

Date/Time	Odometer		Total Mileage	Destination	Notes
	Start	End			

Year:________________ Make:________________ Model:________________

Date/Time	Odometer		Total Mileage	Destination	Notes
	Start	End			

Year:________________ Make:________________ Model:________________

Date/Time	Odometer		Total Mileage	Destination	Notes
	Start	End			

Year:________________ Make:________________ Model:________________

Date/Time	Odometer		Total Mileage	Destination	Notes
	Start	End			

Year:________________ Make:________________ Model:________________

Date/Time	Odometer		Total Mileage	Destination	Notes
	Start	End			

Year:________________ Make:________________ Model:________________

Date/Time	Odometer		Total Mileage	Destination	Notes
	Start	End			

Year:________________ Make:________________ Model:________________

Date/Time	Odometer		Total Mileage	Destination	Notes
	Start	End			

Year:________________ Make:________________ Model:________________

Date/Time	Odometer		Total Mileage	Destination	Notes
	Start	End			

Year:________________ Make:________________ Model:________________

Date/Time	Odometer		Total Mileage	Destination	Notes
	Start	End			

Year:________________ Make:________________ Model:________________

Date/Time	Odometer		Total Mileage	Destination	Notes
	Start	End			

Year:________________ Make:________________ Model:________________

Date/Time	Odometer		Total Mileage	Destination	Notes
	Start	End			

Year:_______________ Make:_______________ Model:_______________

Date/Time	Odometer		Total Mileage	Destination	Notes
	Start	End			

Year:________________ Make:________________ Model:________________

Date/Time	Odometer		Total Mileage	Destination	Notes
	Start	End			

Year:________________ Make:________________ Model:________________

Date/Time	Odometer		Total Mileage	Destination	Notes
	Start	End			

Year:________________ Make:________________ Model:________________

Date/Time	Odometer		Total Mileage	Destination	Notes
	Start	End			

Year:________________ Make:________________ Model:________________

Date/Time	Odometer		Total Mileage	Destination	Notes
	Start	End			

Year:________________ Make:________________ Model:________________

Date/Time	Odometer		Total Mileage	Destination	Notes
	Start	End			

Year:________________ Make:________________ Model:________________

Date/Time	Odometer		Total Mileage	Destination	Notes
	Start	End			

Year:________________ Make:________________ Model:________________

Date/Time	Odometer		Total Mileage	Destination	Notes
	Start	End			

Year:________________ Make:________________ Model:________________

Date/Time	Odometer		Total Mileage	Destination	Notes
	Start	End			

Year:____________ Make:____________ Model:____________

Date/Time	Odometer		Total Mileage	Destination	Notes
	Start	End			

Year:________________ Make:________________ Model:________________

Date/Time	Odometer		Total Mileage	Destination	Notes
	Start	End			

Year:________________ Make:________________ Model:________________

Date/Time	Odometer		Total Mileage	Destination	Notes
	Start	End			

Year:________________ Make:________________ Model:________________

Date/Time	Odometer		Total Mileage	Destination	Notes
	Start	End			

Year:________________ Make:________________ Model:________________

Date/Time	Odometer		Total Mileage	Destination	Notes
	Start	End			

Year:________________ Make:________________ Model:________________

Date/Time	Odometer		Total Mileage	Destination	Notes
	Start	End			

Year:________________ Make:________________ Model:________________

Date/Time	Odometer		Total Mileage	Destination	Notes
	Start	End			

Year:________________ Make:________________ Model:________________

Date/Time	Odometer		Total Mileage	Destination	Notes
	Start	End			

Year:____________ Make:____________ Model:____________

Date/Time	Odometer		Total Mileage	Destination	Notes
	Start	End			

Year:__________________ Make:__________________ Model:__________________

Date/Time	Odometer		Total Mileage	Destination	Notes
	Start	End			

Year:________________ Make:________________ Model:________________

Date/Time	Odometer		Total Mileage	Destination	Notes
	Start	End			

Year:________________ Make:________________ Model:________________

Date/Time	Odometer		Total Mileage	Destination	Notes
	Start	End			

Year:________________ Make:________________ Model:________________

Date/Time	Odometer		Total Mileage	Destination	Notes
	Start	End			

Year:________________ Make:________________ Model:________________

Date/Time	Odometer		Total Mileage	Destination	Notes
	Start	End			

Year:________________ Make:________________ Model:________________

Date/Time	Odometer		Total Mileage	Destination	Notes
	Start	End			

Year:_______________ Make:_______________ Model:_______________

Date/Time	Odometer		Total Mileage	Destination	Notes
	Start	End			

Year:________________ Make:________________ Model:________________

Date/Time	Odometer		Total Mileage	Destination	Notes
	Start	End			

Year:________________ Make:________________ Model:________________

Date/Time	Odometer		Total Mileage	Destination	Notes
	Start	End			

Year:________________ Make:________________ Model:________________

Date/Time	Odometer		Total Mileage	Destination	Notes
	Start	End			

Year:________________ Make:________________ Model:________________

Date/Time	Odometer		Total Mileage	Destination	Notes
	Start	End			

Year:________________ Make:________________ Model:________________

Date/Time	Odometer		Total Mileage	Destination	Notes
	Start	End			

Year:________________ Make:________________ Model:________________

Date/Time	Odometer		Total Mileage	Destination	Notes
	Start	End			

Year:________________ Make:________________ Model:________________

Date/Time	Odometer		Total Mileage	Destination	Notes
	Start	End			

Year:__________ Make:__________ Model:__________

Date/Time	Odometer		Total Mileage	Destination	Notes
	Start	End			

Year:________________ Make:________________ Model:________________

Date/Time	Odometer		Total Mileage	Destination	Notes
	Start	End			

Year:________________ Make:________________ Model:________________

Date/Time	Odometer		Total Mileage	Destination	Notes
	Start	End			

Year:________________ Make:________________ Model:________________

Date/Time	Odometer		Total Mileage	Destination	Notes
	Start	End			

Year:__________ Make:__________ Model:__________

Date/Time	Odometer		Total Mileage	Destination	Notes
	Start	End			

Year:________________ Make:________________ Model:________________

Date/Time	Odometer		Total Mileage	Destination	Notes
	Start	End			

Year:________________ Make:________________ Model:________________

Date/Time	Odometer		Total Mileage	Destination	Notes
	Start	End			

Year:__________ Make:__________ Model:__________

Date/Time	Odometer		Total Mileage	Destination	Notes
	Start	End			

Year:__________ Make:__________ Model:__________

Date/Time	Odometer		Total Mileage	Destination	Notes
	Start	End			

Year:________________ Make:________________ Model:________________

Date/Time	Odometer		Total Mileage	Destination	Notes
	Start	End			

Year:________________ Make:________________ Model:________________

Date/Time	Odometer		Total Mileage	Destination	Notes
	Start	End			

Year:________________ Make:________________ Model:________________

Date/Time	Odometer		Total Mileage	Destination	Notes
	Start	End			

Year:________________ Make:________________ Model:________________

Date/Time	Odometer		Total Mileage	Destination	Notes
	Start	End			

Year:________________ Make:________________ Model:________________

Date/Time	Odometer		Total Mileage	Destination	Notes
	Start	End			

Year:________________ Make:________________ Model:________________

Date/Time	Odometer		Total Mileage	Destination	Notes
	Start	End			

Year:__________________ Make:__________________ Model:__________________

Date/Time	Odometer		Total Mileage	Destination	Notes
	Start	End			

Year:________________ Make:________________ Model:________________

Date/Time	Odometer		Total Mileage	Destination	Notes
	Start	End			

Year:________________ Make:________________ Model:________________

Date/Time	Odometer		Total Mileage	Destination	Notes
	Start	End			

Year:________________ Make:________________ Model:________________

Date/Time	Odometer		Total Mileage	Destination	Notes
	Start	End			

Year:________________ Make:________________ Model:________________

Date/Time	Odometer		Total Mileage	Destination	Notes
	Start	End			

Year:________________ Make:________________ Model:________________

Date/Time	Odometer		Total Mileage	Destination	Notes
	Start	End			

Year:________________ Make:________________ Model:________________

Date/Time	Odometer		Total Mileage	Destination	Notes
	Start	End			

Year:________________ Make:________________ Model:________________

Date/Time	Odometer		Total Mileage	Destination	Notes
	Start	End			

Year:________________ Make:________________ Model:________________

Date/Time	Odometer		Total Mileage	Destination	Notes
	Start	End			

Year:________________ Make:________________ Model:________________

Date/Time	Odometer		Total Mileage	Destination	Notes
	Start	End			

Year:________________ Make:________________ Model:________________

Date/Time	Odometer		Total Mileage	Destination	Notes
	Start	End			

Year:________________ Make:________________ Model:________________

Date/Time	Odometer		Total Mileage	Destination	Notes
	Start	End			

Year:________________ Make:________________ Model:________________

Date/Time	Odometer		Total Mileage	Destination	Notes
	Start	End			

Year:________________ Make:________________ Model:________________

Date/Time	Odometer		Total Mileage	Destination	Notes
	Start	End			

Year:________________ Make:________________ Model:________________

Date/Time	Odometer		Total Mileage	Destination	Notes
	Start	End			

Year:_______________ Make:_______________ Model:_______________

Date/Time	Odometer		Total Mileage	Destination	Notes
	Start	End			

Year:________________ Make:________________ Model:________________

Date/Time	Odometer		Total Mileage	Destination	Notes
	Start	End			

Year:________________ Make:________________ Model:________________

Date/Time	Odometer		Total Mileage	Destination	Notes
	Start	End			

Year:________________ Make:________________ Model:________________

Date/Time	Odometer		Total Mileage	Destination	Notes
	Start	End			

Year:__________ Make:__________ Model:__________

Date/Time	Odometer		Total Mileage	Destination	Notes
	Start	End			

Year:________________ Make:________________ Model:________________

Date/Time	Odometer		Total Mileage	Destination	Notes
	Start	End			

Year:________________ Make:________________ Model:________________

Date/Time	Odometer		Total Mileage	Destination	Notes
	Start	End			

Year:__________________ Make:__________________ Model:__________________

Date/Time	Odometer		Total Mileage	Destination	Notes
	Start	End			

Year:________________ Make:________________ Model:________________

Date/Time	Odometer		Total Mileage	Destination	Notes
	Start	End			

Year:____________ Make:____________ Model:____________

Date/Time	Odometer		Total Mileage	Destination	Notes
	Start	End			

Year:____________ Make:____________ Model:____________

Date/Time	Odometer		Total Mileage	Destination	Notes
	Start	End			

Year:________________ Make:________________ Model:________________

Date/Time	Odometer		Total Mileage	Destination	Notes
	Start	End			

Year:________________ Make:________________ Model:________________

Date/Time	Odometer		Total Mileage	Destination	Notes
	Start	End			

Year:__________________ Make:__________________ Model:__________________

Date/Time	Odometer		Total Mileage	Destination	Notes
	Start	End			

Year:__________________ Make:__________________ Model:__________________

Date/Time	Odometer		Total Mileage	Destination	Notes
	Start	End			

Year:______________ Make:______________ Model:______________

Date/Time	Odometer		Total Mileage	Destination	Notes
	Start	End			

Year:________________ Make:________________ Model:________________

Date/Time	Odometer		Total Mileage	Destination	Notes
	Start	End			

Year:________________ Make:________________ Model:________________

Date/Time	Odometer		Total Mileage	Destination	Notes
	Start	End			

Year:________________ Make:________________ Model:________________

Date/Time	Odometer		Total Mileage	Destination	Notes
	Start	End			

Year:________________ Make:________________ Model:________________

Date/Time	Odometer		Total Mileage	Destination	Notes
	Start	End			

Made in United States
Troutdale, OR
07/19/2023

11322427R00066